T
Choc
Ha

The Secret Chocolate Lover's Handbook

Caroline Archer

Illustrated by
Rowan Barnes-Murphy

RED FOX

A Red Fox Book
Published by Random Century Children's Books
20 Vauxhall Bridge Road, London SW1V 2SA

A division of the Random Century Group

London Melbourne Sydney Auckland
Johannesburg and agencies throughout the world

Red Fox edition 1991
Reprinted 1991

Set in Century Schoolbook
by JH Graphics Ltd, Reading

Printed and bound in Great Britain by
Cox & Wyman Ltd, Reading, Berkshire

ISBN 0 09 973490 7

Contents

Introduction

Everybody loves chocolate — it's the favourite sweet all over the world. Whether your personal favourite is a scrumptious box of chocolates, a delicious chocolate bar or yummy chocolate drops, in milk or plain chocolate, then this is the book for you. You'll find it chock-full of fascinating and funny chocolatey things. There are amazing facts, jokes, mouth-watering chocolate recipes which are delicious but easy to make, amusing chocolate games to play, chocolate tongue-twisters and funny book titles, a chocolate quiz and chocolate puzzles. And on page 104 you'll find a chocolate survey where you can list your own favourite chocolate bars, secretly record your chocolate-eating habits and note down your own favourite recipes.

Happy chocolate eating!

1
Chocolate Truths

Real chocolate lovers need to be armed with the facts! So here, to start you off, is an amazing collection of information about chocolate, from the amount we eat to statistics on your favourite chocolate bars and why it's good for you!

- The United Kingdom has the third highest total comsumption of chocolate per person in the world. The countries that eat the most are Switzerland, followed by Norway. But if you include other types of sweets as well as chocolates, then the United Kingdom has the highest consumption in the world!

- The average confectionery consumption per person in the United Kingdom is 254 grammes per person per week.

- Almost 75 per cent of the population of the United Kingdom eat bars of chocolate every week.

- On average, each person in the United Kingdom spends £1.04 each week on confectionery.

- Over 75 per cent of the population of the United Kingdom buy boxes of chocolates or

chocolate assortments, but only a small proportion of people – the real chocolate addicts – buy more than one of these a month.

- On average, children eat a confectionery product once a day and adults once every two days.

- Britain's best-selling chocolate bars stack up like this:

    No.1 Kit Kat
           Mars Bar
    No.2 Cadbury's Dairy Milk
           Twix
    No. 3 Quality Street
           Maltesers
           Roses
           Wispa

No.4 Bounty
Cadbury's Fruit & Nut
Cadbury's Whole Nut
Chunky Aero
Crunchie
Flake
Snickers
Milk Tray
Milky Way

- It takes the whole of one year's crop from one tree to make half a kilo of cocoa.

- In Italy people used to eat pasta made of chocolate. In Venice today there is a shop where you can still buy cocoa-flavoured pasta.

- When chocolate was first used in cooking it was added to savoury dishes. Recipes still exist for turkey in chilli and chocolate sauce, duck with chocolate, chilli con carne with chocolate, wild boar with chocolate sauce, and braised pigeon with chocolate.

- In 1988 8,288 tonnes of Smarties were sold in the United Kingdom. That's the equivalent of 8,886 billion individual Smarties! And it means that 282 Smarties were eaten every second, or 16,925 every minute. That's an awful lot of Smarties.

- If all the Smarties eaten in 1988 were laid end to end, they would stretch over 102,353 kilometres. If they were put into tubes and the tubes were laid end to end, they would stretch over 28,567 kilometres. And if the Smarties were laid out next to each other, they would cover an area of 4.5 square kilometres.

- Kit Kats were first made in 1935. They were called Rowntree's Chocolate Crisp, but then two years later the name was changed to Kit Kat. No one knows where the name Kit Kat came from but it might have been taken from a famous 1920's club which was called the Kit Kat Club.

- Over 3.5 million Kit Kat bars are made every day. Around 1300 million bars are sold each year.

- Kit Kat wrappers haven't changed much since 1937. They have always been red and white, with the familiar oval shape on the front.

- You might be surprised to know how old some of your favourite chocolates are — or rather, when they were first made. In fact, many of the most popular brands are over fifty years old, as this list shows.

  Cadbury's Dairy Milk 1905
  Bournville plain chocolate 1910
  Black Magic 1933
  Aero 1935
  Kit Kat 1935
  Dairy Box 1936
  Quality Street 1936
  Rolos and Smarties 1937
  After Eights 1962
  Toffee Crisp 1963
  Yorkie 1976

- Over two billion Quality Street sweets are made at the Rowntree Mackintosh factory at Halifax in Yorkshire every year.

- Quality Street was named after a play of the same name by J. M. Barrie, who wrote *Peter Pan*. Two of the characters in the play are called Major Quality and Miss Sweetly.

- Only three centres in the Black Magic assortment have ever been changed.

- The Cadbury's Bournville site alone produces 1,500 tonnes of chocolate a week — 1.6 million bars of various kinds, plus 50 million Hazelnut Whirls, Almond Clusters and other individual chocolates.

● Enough Cadbury's Dairy Milk chocolate is sold each year to cover all the football pitches in the Football League.

● When Cadbury's were trying to think of a name for Dairy Milk in 1905, three names were considered – Jersey, Highland Milk and Dairymaid. Dairymaid was changed to Dairy Milk, and the chocolate has been called that ever since.

● Wispa bars are produced with such precision that the size of the tiny air bubbles in the chocolate is controlled to within 0.2–0.3mm. The temperature is monitored at 1,000 points along the production line, and there are over twenty kilometres of electric cable in the control system for the bars.

● The Cadbury's Creme Egg plant, which cost £14 million to set up, can produce 270 million eggs a year at the rate of 1,100 per minute.

● Rowntree estimates that as much as 70 per cent of all confectionery purchases are made on impulse. Although adults buy 91 per cent of confectionery, they only eat 64 per cent; children eat the remaining 36 per cent.

● The town of Derry Church, Pennsylvania in the United States was re-named Hershey in 1906 after Milton Hershey, who set up a chocolate factory there. The Hershey company makes the Reese's Pieces that featured in the film *E.T.*

- Hershey's Kisses are another of their products – little drop-shaped chocolates individually wrapped in silver foil. Thirty-three million Hershey's Kisses are produced every day.

- 1973 saw the opening of 'Hershey's Chocolate World' – a theme park entirely devoted to chocolate. Among other attractions are people walking around dressed up as life-sized chocolate bars.

- As long as you don't overdo it, chocolate can be good for you. For example, a 40g milk chocolate bar supplies more protein, calcium and riboflavin than a banana, a carrot, an orange or an apple or an equivalent amount of raisins by weight. Milk chocolate also contains vitamins A and B.

- The U.S. Food and Drug Administration has scientific evidence to prove that chocolate neither causes nor aggravates acne.

- Chocolate has been included in the foods provided on all American and Russian space flights because it is a morale booster that also provides nutrients.

- Chocolate sculpture competitions are frequently held in the United States. Nine thousand chocolate artists entered one such competition in San Francisco in the early 1980s.

- The big department stores in Tokyo, Japan often celebrate Valentine's day with chocolate, carving huge statues entirely out of white chocolate.

- According to *The Guinness Book of Records*, the largest chocolate model ever made was of the 1992 Olympic Centre in Barcelona. Completed in 1985, the model weighed 1800 kg and was 10 metres long.

- Real chocolate addicts in the UK can indulge themselves by going on special chocoholics' weekends organized in an Oxfordshire hotel. The whole two days are devoted to chocolate in one way or another. Meals consist of chocolate in various forms, such as chocolate croissants

14

for breakfast and venison with blackcurrant and chocolate sauce for dinner, there are talks about the history of chocolate, and organized tours of a chocolate factory. Survival kits of extra chocolate bars are left in the bedrooms in case people feel peckish, though unfortunately even the most devoted chocolate addicts soon start to feel queasy after so much of their favourite sweet!

• In the USA, each year several hundred thousand Americans attend 'chocolate weekends'. Dances are held where you have to dress up as your favourite chocolate. At one of these weekends, held at Miami's Fontainebleau Hilton Hotel, guests were allowed to dunk actor Don Johnson into a huge 2,700-litre tank of chocolate syrup! The story has it that he survived the experience!

2
Crazy Chocolate Chuckles

Here are lots of chocolatey chuckles about everyone's favourite confectionery!

CUSTOMER: Why is my chocolate cake so dirty and mushed up?
WAITRESS: *Well, you did ask me to step on it!*

How did Frankenstein eat his chocolate ice cream?
He bolted it down.

Knock, Knock.
Who's there!
Sharon.
Sharon Who?
Sharon share alike — give me some of your Mars bar.

HUSBAND: Shall I offer this tramp a piece of my chocolate sponge cake?
WIFE: *Why, what harm has he done us?*

What's the difference between teachers and chocolate eclairs!
People like chocolate eclairs.

NEWSFLASH: A lorry carrying chocolate spread has collided with a car on the M6. Police are advising motorists to stick to their own lanes.

What did the vampire say when her boyfriend gave her a box of chocolates!
Fangs very much

Did you hear about the chocolate blancmange fish? It set!

If you put a group of professors in a London Underground train, what have you got!
A tube of Smarties.

JANE: Chocolate was the cause of my mother's death.
SUE: *You mean she ate too much?*
JANE: No, a box of chocolate bars fell on her head.

Knock, knock.
Who's there?
Harriet.
Harriet who?
Harriet a whole box of chocolates!

Charlie was given two bars of chocolate, a big one and a small one, by his granny, and told to share them with his sister Lucy. He gave the small one to Lucy, and ate the big one himself.

'That's not fair!' said Lucy. 'If Granny had given them to me, I'd have given you the big one and kept the small one for myself.'

What do goblins make chocolate cake with?
Elf-raising flour.

PATIENT: Doctor, doctor, I feel like a bar of chocolate.
DOCTOR: *Well, come over here − I won't bite you!*

What's chocolate outside, peanut inside and sings hymns?
A Sunday School Treet!

Knock, knock.
Who's there?
May.
May who?
May I have a chocolate egg, please?

CUSTOMER: Is there any chocolate sponge on this menu?
WAITRESS: *No, madam, I wiped it off.*

What's red, crunchy and wears sunglasses?
A Smartie on holiday!

JUDGE: Order, order in the court!
PRISONER: *I'll have a chocolate milk-shake please.*

How can you prevent chocolate from going bad?
By eating it!

PAT: Which hand do you stir your drinking chocolate with?
MICK: *I don't stir it with my hand — I use a spoon!*

What's the difference between a schoolteacher and a train!
A schoolteacher says, 'Take that chocolate out of your mouth!' A train says 'Choo! choo!'

PATIENT: Doctor, doctor, I get a stabbing pain in my eye every time I drink a cup of cocoa.
DOCTOR: *Have you tried taking the spoon out of the cup first?*

CUSTOMER: Waiter, what's this insect doing in my chocolate mousse?
WAITER: *Trying to get out!*

Knock, knock.
Who's there?
Bernardette.
Bernardette who?
Bernardette all my chocolates!

How do you get an elephant into a box of chocolate raisins?
Take out the chocolate raisins first.

JUDGE: You claim you robbed the sweetshop because you were starving. So why didn't you take the chocolates and sweets instead of the cash out of the till?
ACCUSED: *I'm a proud man, Your Honour, and I make it a rule to pay for everything I eat.*

CUSTOMER: Waiter, waiter, there's a dead fly in my hot chocolate.
WAITER: *Well, what do you expect for 50p — a live one?*

3
The Story of Chocolate

Chocolate was originally discovered by Indians of Central and South America. About 500 years ago the Aztecs of Mexico and the Incas of Peru discovered that seeds of the cacao, or cocoa, trees that grew wild in the jungle could be made into a delicious drink. They made their drinking chocolate by roasting and crushing the cacao beans,

then putting them in a large jug and whisking them up with water, vanilla and spices. The Aztec name for this drink was *Chocolatl*, and they called the cacoa tree *Cacauatl*. Our names chocolate and cocoa come from these words.

The Aztecs believed that the cacao trees were a gift from the gods – and our scientific name for cocoa, *Theobroma cacao*, means 'food of the gods.' They made religious offerings of jugs of chocolate in thanks, and used chocolate at many of their religious ceremonies such as wedding feasts, the naming of babies, and funerals, when chocolate was drunk and cocoa beans were offered to the gods. Cups of chocolate were served to guests, and given to brave fighters, but not to cowards. The Aztecs also used cocoa beans as money; a pumpkin might have cost four beans, and a rabbit ten beans.

The explorer Christopher Columbus was the first person to bring chocolate back from Central America. But in 1502, when he introduced cocoa beans to the court of Spain, neither King Ferdinand nor anyone else showed any interest.

Some twenty years later, the Spanish explorer Hernando Cortez conquered Mexico. Montezuma, the Aztec ruler at the time, was a real chocolate addict; it is said that he sometimes drank chocolate 50 times a day, served in cups of pure gold. It was Montezuma who gave Cortez his first drink of chocolate, and he came to like it. He ordered that his galleons should be loaded with cocoa beans, and shipped them back to Spain. On the way home the explorers called at Africa where they planted some cocoa trees from Mexican seeds, for future use.

This time the drink became popular with the Spanish nobility and rich people — it was expensive so not everyone could afford to buy it. It was served hot, flavoured with cinnamon, vanilla and sugar.

The recipe for making drinking chocolate remained a closely-guarded Spanish secret for nearly one hundred years. Then gradually the secret began to spread to other European countries, carried by travellers. Smugglers began to trade in cocoa beans, as well as other contraband goods. In 1660 the Spanish princess Marie Theresa married the French king Louis XIV and this helped to make the drink popular in France.

In London and other cities 'chocolate houses' were opened in the 1660s. These were smart places where people met to sit and talk and enjoy the new drink, which remained an expensive luxury. In Great Britain, cocoa cost six shillings and eightpence a pound. In 1664 Samuel Pepys, the famous diary-writer, wrote that he 'Went to Mr Bland's and there drank my morning draft of good chocollatte.'

By the early 1700s chocolate had become more like the drink we know today, served hot and with milk added to it instead of, or as well as, water.

As more and more people began to enjoy drinking chocolate, more cocoa trees were planted, in plantations in the West Indies, the Far East and Africa. This was the beginning of the cocoa industry which is so important to many countries today.

The price of chocolate stayed high in Britain until 1853, when import taxes on cocoa were reduced. This meant that more people could now afford to buy it and enjoy the delicious drink.

Until the early 1800s, chocolate had only been available as a drink. However, throughout Europe, people were experimenting with ways of making solid 'eating' chocolate, and in 1847 the English company Fry and Sons introduced their first bar of chocolate. Thirty years later, in Switzerland, milk was first added to chocolate. Chocolate-making processes have been greatly improved since those days, with companies around the world manufacturing a delicious assortment of chocolates and chocolate bars.

4
How Chocolate is Made

The bean

Chocolate, as we have seen, begins life as a cocoa bean. These beans grow in large pods on the trunks of cacao, or cocoa, trees, in tropical countries such as Central and South America and Ghana in West Africa. Seeds from the cocoa bean are dried and then ground into a dark brown powder called cocoa. Cocoa can be made into drinks – cocoa and drinking chocolate – or into chocolate. So that's where the delicious sweet comes from!

The tree

Cacao trees grow to a height of 5 metres or more, and look rather like apple trees. They are planted in rich soil, in the shade of taller trees such as bananas, rubber or breadfruit, for protection. They have thin, shiny, evergreen leaves, which measure up to 30 centimetres long. Thousands of delicate pinkish-white flowers grow directly on the tree's trunk and main branches. Some of these develop into a fruit, called a cocoa pod, which can be up to 15 to 20 centimetres long and looks like a long melon. As the pods ripen they change from green to a golden yellow, orange or red colour.

Inside each pod are between twenty and fifty purple cocoa beans set in a white pulp. If you ate a bean at this stage you would find it very bitter-tasting and not very nice — it has to undergo several different processes before it becomes delicious cocoa or chocolate.

Many beans are needed to produce one tin of cocoa or one bar of chocolate, so cocoa is quite expensive to buy.

Growing

Cacao trees grow best in hot, wet countries either side of the Equator, between the Tropic of Cancer and the Tropic of Capricorn. Originally the trees grew only in the forests of Central and South America, but seeds have been taken to many other parts of the world, where the trees now grow, such as Ghana, Nigeria and the Ivory Coast on the west coast of Africa, as well as Sri Lanka, Malaysia, Indonesia, the Philippines, Papua New Guinea and the Fiji Islands. In Central and South America the trees grow in Mexico, Costa Rica, Panama, Venezuela, Colombia, Ecuador, Peru and Brazil. Caribbean countries where the trees grow include Jamaica, Cuba, Haiti, the Dominican Republic, Grenada and Trinidad and Tobago.

Harvesting

Cocoa is grown on cocoa farms. Some small farms are owned by families, while other farms are large plantations owned by big companies and employing hundreds of workers.

At harvest time on small farms all the members of the family, together with relatives and friends, help to harvest the cocoa beans. The pods are cut from the tree with long sharp knives known as machetes or cutlasses. The pods are then piled up high, and split open carefully one by one so the precious beans are not damaged.

The cocoa beans and pulp are scooped out of the pods, heaped up on huge plantain leaves and covered with more leaves, or stacked in boxes. The heat causes the beans to ferment, which develops the real chocolate flavour and turns the beans brown. The pulp becomes liquid and drains away.

After about a week, when the beans have all fermented, they are dried. They are spread out on the ground, or on long trestle tables, to dry in the sun. In wet countries, drying machines blow hot air through the beans. They have to be kept out of the rain otherwise they will rot.

Exporting

When the beans have dried, they are put into sacks, taken to collection centres or buying stations, and sold. They are then transported to the nearest port, loaded on to ships and sent to factories in other countries where they are turned into cocoa powder, cocoa and chocolate.

Cleaning and roasting

When cocoa beans reach Great Britain from the countries where they are grown, they are transported to processing factories. There they are cleaned to remove dust, leaves and stones, then roasted for about an hour in a machine called a continuous roaster. This is a revolving drum through which hot air passes as the beans move along it. The roasting process develops the flavour of the cocoa beans, which now begin to smell like chocolate.

Kibbling, winnowing and grinding

The roasted beans are then kibbled, or broken up into small pieces, and then winnowing takes place – the brittle shell or husk is blown away, leaving the centres of the beans, known as the nibs.

The cocoa nibs are poured into grinding mills, where they are ground between steel rollers and turned into a chocolate-coloured paste, rather like thick cream, called cocoa mass.

Cocoa mass and cocoa butter

Cocoa mass is the basic ingredient for all cocoa and chocolate products. It contains a lot of cocoa butter, which is a very oily substance. About half of the cocoa butter has to be removed from the mass before good cocoa or chocolate can be made. It is pressed out, leaving a solid block of hard cocoa.

Making cocoa and drinking chocolate

These blocks are ground to a fine powder in a crushing mill, producing cocoa powder. This is then sieved and either poured straight into tins or mixed with fine sugar to make drinking chocolate. The tins are labelled, packed and transported to the shops to be sold.

Making milk chocolate

Milk and plain eating chocolate are made by different processes. Both these processes are controlled very carefully to make sure that the chocolate turns out exactly as it should do.

Milk chocolate was invented in 1876 by a Swiss man called Daniel Peter. Since then it has become very popular. This is how it is made today.

Cocoa mass is sent to a chocolate-making factory where it is mixed with sugar and fresh cream milk. The milk does not mix easily with the rich cocoa butter which remains in the mass, so it has to be condensed first before being added to the cocoa mass. The mixture is then dried in vacuum ovens, and becomes milk chocolate crumb.

The chocolate crumb is ground between huge rollers and turned into paste, then extra cocoa butter is put back in and chocolate flavourings are added. Colouring is not necessary because of the attractive natural chocolatey colour.

The next stage in the process is called conching. The chocolate paste is poured into a conche machine, where it is pounded with heavy rollers for many hours, to make it really smooth and full of flavour. At the end of this process, fruit and nuts are added to the mixture if required.

When the chocolate is a smooth liquid, it is poured into shaped moulds and cooled carefully, or tempered, until it sets hard.

When it has set it is removed from the moulds and machine-wrapped. Aluminium foil helps to keep the chocolate in good condition, and a colourful paper wrapper protects it further.

Making plain chocolate

At the chocolate-making factory cocoa mass is mixed with extra cocoa butter and sugar, then ground, conched and tempered in the same way as milk chocolate.

Boxes and bars

To make filled chocolates to go in boxes, the liquid chocolate is moulded or poured on to the chocolate centres, then cooled. To make bars of chocolate, the liquid chocolate is poured into bar-shaped moulds.

Chocolate factories

These are very modern and scientific places. They usually operate all day and night, seven days a week, with workers on shifts. Over 1,600 chocolate bars a minute can be produced on one machine, and 800 chocolate bars a minute can be wrapped by a chocolate-wrapping machine. Chocolate boxes used to be filled by hand, but this is now done by machine.

The story of Smarties

Now, let's look at one particular chocolate, and see how Smarties are made.

First of all, melted milk chocolate is poured between two very cold metal rollers. The surface of these rollers is covered with dimples, and when the rollers turn against each other the dimples meet to form the rounded shape of Smarties.

The chocolate starts to harden against the cold metal rollers, and is cooled further until the Smartie centres are completely hard.

The Smartie centres are then poured into a revolving drum and rubbed together, which smooths the rough edges.

The next stage is to apply the crisp sugar shell to the milk chocolate centres. This process is called 'drum coating'. The centres are poured into another drum, and liquid and dry ingredients are added in stages. These coat the centres. In between the various coatings, the Smarties are gradually dried out with warm air. When the centres are evenly coated, further coloured sugar coatings are added.

The final stage is polishing, when the Smarties are given their shiny appearance.

Each Smartie colour is made separately. When they are finished, the different colours are mixed together in even numbers. Machines then pack them into tubes and cartons, ready to be taken to the shops and sold.

5
Crazier Chocolate Chuckles

Have you heard the joke about the ants and the box of chocolate biscuits? You'll find it in this chapter, together with lots more chocolatey chortles.

Why did the ants run along the box of chocolate biscuits?
Because the instructions said 'Tear along the dotted line!'

What do you get when you cross a cow, a sheep and a goat?
A milky bar kid!

Knock, Knock
Who's there!
Henrietta and Juliet.
Henrietta and Juliet who?
Henrietta whole box of chocolates and feels ill.
Juliet some too but she feels OK.

What's the difference between an elephant and a bar of chocolate?
Have you ever tried to take the wrapper off an elephant?

A young girl all bright and breezy
Said that eating chocolates was easy.
After downing fifteen
Her face went bright green,
And she looked and felt terribly queasy!

MRS HIGGINBOTTOM: We're having Mother for tea, dear.
MR HIGGINBOTTOM: *Oh dear! I'd much rather have a nice piece of chocolate cake.*

What should you do if you find a blue chocolate?
Try to cheer it up.

Why did the Easter egg go into the jungle?
Because it was an eggsplorer.

Could you kill somebody just by throwing Easter eggs at him?
Yes, he would be eggs-terminated.

A COCONUT — someone who is crazy about hot chocolate.

MOTHER: Come in, Sandra, and I'll give you some chocolate biscuits. Are your feet dirty?
SANDRA: *Yes, Mum, but I've got my shoes on.*

NEWSFLASH! The Common Market Commissioners' plan to have all chocolates wrapped in tin has been foiled.

Knock, knock.
Who's there?
Noah.
Noah who?
Noah don't want a box of chocolates, thanks.

FELICITY: Whenever I'm down in the dumps I get myself a new box of chocolates.
GWENDOLINE: *Oh, so that's where you get them!*

CUSTOMER: I can't eat this disgusting chocolate cake. Call the manager!
WAITER: *It's no good, sir — he can't eat it either.*

BILL: Do you feel just like a cup of cocoa?
BEN: *Oh, yes*
BILL: I thought so — you look sloppy, wet and hot!

Knock, knock
Who's there?
Ivor.
Ivor who?
Ivor you let me have a bar of chocolate or I'll cry.

What's large, brown and has a soft centre?
A chocolate-coated elephant.

How do you know if an elephant has been at your box of chocolates?
By the giant footsteps in the coffee creme.

Have you heard the joke about the smashed chocolate biscuits! It's pretty crumby.

KYLIE: I'll give this bag of chocolate raisins to anyone who is quite happy.
JASON: *I'm quite happy.*
KYLIE: Then why do you want my bag of chocolate raisins?

SAILOR SAM: I was once shipwrecked in the middle of the ocean and had to live for a week on a bar of chocolate.
NAUGHTY NIGEL: *Good job you didn't fall off!*

CUSTOMER: Waiter, waiter, how long will my chocolate cake be?
WAITER: *We don't do long cakes, sir — just round ones.*

Knock, knock
Who's there?
Romeo.
Romeo who?
Romeover to the shore; I want to go and buy a chocolate eclair.

CUSTOMER: Waiter, waiter, there's a fly on my chocolate blancmange!
WAITER: *Don't worry, madam — there's a spider on your spoon.*

PATIENT: Doctor, doctor, I keep thinking I'm a pound coin!
DOCTOR: *Well, go and buy some chocolate – the change should do you good.*

GEORGE: It looks like rain.
GEORGINA: *I know it does, but it says chocolate instant whip on the packet.*

Knock, knock.
Who's there?
Don.
Don who?
Don mess about – give me a bar of chocolate!

CUSTOMER: Waiter, waiter, why have you got your thumb on my chocolate cake?
WAITER: *Well, madam, I don't want to drop it on the floor again.*

6
Yum yum! Scrumptious Chocolate Recipes

Next time you're feeling peckish, try some of these delicious chocolate recipes – they're guaranteed to make your mouth water!

No-bake Chocolate Cake

This delicious cake doesn't need to be baked, so it's very easy to make. Ask an adult for help with melting the chocolate.

Ingredients
300g digestive biscuits
100g unsalted butter or margarine
2 level tablespoons cocoa powder
6 level tablespoons golden syrup
knob of butter or margarine
about 500cl of water
100g plain chocolate, broken into pieces
about 24 walnuts halves or hazelnuts
(You will also need one 20-cm round sandwich
    tin.)

Method
1 Put the digestive biscuits into a clean plastic
bag. Squeeze out the air then seal the bag with a
wire tie or elastic band. Crush the biscuits into
small pieces by rolling a rolling pin over them.
2 Put the butter or margarine, cocoa powder and
golden syrup into a large saucepan. (If you put the
golden syrup tin into a warm oven half an hour
before you are going to measure it out, it will be
easier to handle but use an oven glove when you
are taking it out as the tin may get too hot to
hold.) Using a wooden spoon, stir the mixture
over a low heat until the butter has melted. Take
the pan off the heat.
3 Add the crushed biscuits to the mixture and
stir them in.
4 Grease all over the inside of the sandwich tin,
using a piece of kitchen roll or greaseproof paper
and the knob of butter.
5 Spoon the biscuit mixture into the tin, press-
ing it down evenly so it is flat and covers the
bottom of the tin. Put the tin in the fridge and
leave it for at least one hour to set.

6 Pour the water into a small saucepan so it is one-third full. Put the chocolate pieces in a shallow bowl which is the right size to rest on the top of the saucepan. The water should not touch the bottom of the bowl.

7 Sit the bowl on top of the pan and turn on the stove. Let the water heat slowly until the chocolate melts, then take the bowl off the saucepan, holding it with an oven cloth so you don't burn your fingers. Turn off the stove.

8 Rest the sandwich tin containing the cake mixture carefully on the saucepan of hot water for about 10 seconds, so that the butter on the inside of the tin melts. Take the tin off the saucepan.

9 Put a large plate upside down over the cake mixture, and turn the cake and the tin upside down. You should be able to lift the tin gently off the cake. If it sticks a bit, hold both the tin and plate and give them a few careful shakes.

10 Pour the melted chocolate over the cake, using a knife to spread it evenly. Put the nuts around the edge of the cake, with one in the middle. Eat the cake as soon as the chocolate has set.

Chocolate Biscuits

Ask an adult for help with putting these mouth-watering biscuits into the oven and taking them out. You won't need much help with eating them!

Ingredients
knob of butter or margarine
125g plain chocolate

about 500cl of water
125g unsalted butter or margarine
1 egg
175g granulated or soft brown sugar
175g self-raising flour, sifted
(You will also need one non-stick baking sheet.)

Method

1 Turn the oven on to gas 6, 200°C, 400°F.

2 Lightly grease the baking sheet, using a piece of kitchen roll or greaseproof paper and the knob of butter or margarine.

3 Melt the chocolate over a bowl of boiling water, as in the recipe for No-bake Chocolate Cake (see page 39). Leave the chocolate to cool for 5 to 10 minutes. Cut the butter or margarine into small pieces and add to the chocolate. Stir with a wooden spoon until it is mixed smoothly.

4 Break the egg into a bowl. Add the sugar and stir it in with a fork. Mix in the melted chocolate and butter, then add the flour. Mix to a stiff dough, using a wooden spoon.

5 Using your hands, roll the dough into balls each the size of a large walnut. Put the balls on the baking sheet, spaced well apart.

6 Carefully put the baking sheet in the hot oven and bake for 10-12 minutes, until the balls of dough have spread out into round biscuits and the tops are cracked.

7 Wearing oven gloves, carefully take the baking sheet out of the oven. Using a fish slice or spatula, remove the biscuits and put them on a wire rack to cool and go crispy.

Chocolate Crunchy Bars

This is another delectable recipe that doesn't need to be baked in the oven.

Ingredients
knob of butter or margarine
50g unsalted butter or margarine
200g milk or plain chocolate
3 tablespoons golden syrup
225g digestive or rich tea biscuits
icing sugar
(You will also need on 18cm-square shallow baking tin.)

Method
1 Lightly grease the baking tin, using a piece of kitchen roll or greaseproof paper and the knob of butter or margarine.

2 Put the butter or margarine, chocolate and golden syrup into a small saucepan and heat gently. (If you put the golden syrup tin into a warm oven half an hour before you are going to

measure it out, it will be easier to handle
but use oven gloves when you take it out.)
Using a wooden spoon, stir them until they
have melted and are all mixed together.
3 Put the biscuits into a clean plastic bag.
Squeeze out the air then seal the bag with a wire
tie or elastic band. Crush the biscuits into small
pieces by rolling a rolling pin over them.
4 Stir the biscuit pieces into the mixture.
5 Pour the mixture into the baking tin and put
it into the fridge for two to three hours or until
the mixture has set.

6 Cut into bars, using a sharp knife, then turn
them out of the tin. Sift icing sugar lightly over
the top of each bar.

Chocolate Christmas Biscuits

These biscuits are cut into different shapes, such as stars and hearts, and can be hung on the Christmas tree to make unusual decorations. But they taste so good, they might not all last until Christmas Day!

Ingredients
knob of margarine
275g soft margarine
150g caster sugar
1 egg
450g self-raising flour

75g drinking chocolate powder
50g chopped nuts, such as hazelnuts
½ teaspoon cinnamon

(You will also need three non-stick baking trays, approx 30 x 15 cm, some shaped pastry cutters and some strong cotton thread, in green, silver and gold.)

Method
1 Turn on the oven to 190°C, 375°F, gas mark 5.
2 Using the knob of margarine and a piece of kitchen roll, lightly grease the baking trays.
3 Put the margarine, sugar and egg into a large mixing bowl. Beat the mixture, using a wooden spoon, until it is soft and creamy and has changed to a pale yellow colour.
4 Add the flour bit by bit, beating it in with the wooden spoon until it is all mixed in. Then add the drinking chocolate powder, mixing it in well.
5 Gather the mixture together with your hands so it makes a dough and put it on a floured work surface. Roll it into a sausage shape. Cut the sausage into three equal parts, and put two of the pieces of dough aside.
6 Roll out one piece of dough, using a floured rolling pin, until it is about ½cm thick. Using the shaped pastry cutters, cut out shapes from the dough and put them on one of the baking trays. Make holes about 1cm from the top of each shape, using a skewer.
7 Take a second piece of dough. Add the chopped nuts by mixing them in with your hands until they are evenly spread throughout the dough. Then roll out the dough, using a floured rolling pin, until it is about ½cm thick. Using the shaped

pastry cutters, cut out shapes and put them on another baking tray. Make holes in each shape, as above.

8 Take the third piece of dough. Add the cinnamon by mixing it in with your hands until it is evenly spread throughout the dough. Then roll out the dough, cut shapes and make holes as described in step 6.

9 Put three trays into the oven and bake for 12-15 minutes, until the biscuits are firm to the touch. Ask an adult for help with getting the hot trays out of the oven. If the holes in the biscuits have closed up, open them with a skewer.

10 After a minute, remove the biscuits from the baking trays, using a spatula or fish slice, and lay them on a rack to cool.

11 When the biscuits are cold, thread the cotton through the holes and tie it in knots. Hang the biscuits on your Christmas tree and wait for them to be admired!

Chocolate Milk-shake

This is a delicious refreshing drink for hot summer days. The quantity given here is enough for four people.

Ingredients
1 litre of milk
10 dessertspoons of drinking chocolate powder
6 ice cubes
extra drinking chocolate for decoration
(You will also need 4 glasses, 8 straws.)

Method
1 If you have a liquidiser, put all the ingredients into the goblet and liquidise until they have all blended together. Ask an adult to help you with this.
2 If you do not have a liquidiser, pour the milk and drinking chocolate powder into a jug and whisk together until blended. Then add the ice cubes.
3 Pour the mixture into glasses. Decorate by sprinkling half a teaspoonful of drinking chocolate on top of each glass. Serve with straws.

Chocolate Yogurt Cream

This is a delicious pudding which needs to be refrigerated for several hours or overnight before you eat it. The quantity given here makes enough for six people.

Ingredients
250ml natural unsweetened yogurt
250ml double cream
25g chocolate
6 teaspoons soft brown sugar
(You will also need six small dishes, such as small glass bowls.)

Method

1 Pour the yogurt and cream into a large mixing bowl and whip them together, using a whisk, until the mixture is light and quite thick.

2 Using a grater, grate the chocolate and blend it into the mixture.

3 Spoon the mixture into the six small dishes.

4 Sprinkle the top of the mixture with a teaspoonful of soft brown sugar.

5 Put the dishes into the fridge for several hours or overnight. The mixture will set, and the sugar will turn into a scrumptious syrup.

Chocolate Ice Cream

Perfect for summer days, this ice cream needs to be frozen for at least a day before you eat it. Take it out of your freezer an hour before serving and put it into the fridge to make it easier to scoop out of the freezer tray or container.

Ingredients
300ml milk
125g milk chocolate
3 egg yolks
50g granulated sugar
(You will also need a freezer tray or container.)

Method
1 Pour the milk into a saucepan and heat it until it is just boiling (ask an adult for help with this). Then take the pan off the heat.
2 Add the chocolate to the milk. Leave the chocolate to melt and then stir it in using a wooden spoon until it is well blended.
3 Put the egg yolks and sugar into a medium-sized mixing bowl and whisk them until they are pale and thick, using a rotary whisk.
4 Add the chocolate milk to the egg and sugar mixture bit by bit, whisking it in.
5 Pour the mixture into the saucepan. Put it on the cooker on a gentle heat and stir it with a wooden spoon until the mixture thickens and comes up to boiling point (ask an adult for help with this). Don't have the heat too high, and do keep stirring, otherwise the mixture might curdle.
6 When the mixture is thick, take it off the heat and pour it into a freezer tray or container.
7 Put it in the freezer for a day, or until it sets hard.

Chocolate Hedgehog Cake

This is a great cake for a party or special occasion.
It looks just like a spiky hedgehog!

Ingredients
CAKE
vegetable oil
2 level tablespoons cocoa powder
2 tablespoons hot water
100g self raising flour
1 level teaspoon baking powder
2 eggs
100g soft margarine
100g caster sugar
ICING
2 level tablespoons cocoa powder
2 tablespoons hot water
225g icing sugar
75g soft margarine
DECORATION
50g blanched almonds
glacé cherry for nose
2 small sweets for eyes
(You will also need one 20-cm round sandwich
cake tin.

Method
1 Arrange a shelf in the centre of the oven and set
the oven at 170°C, 325°F, gas mark 3.
2 Brush all round the inside of the cake tin with
vegetable oil. Line the base of the tin with a circle
of greaseproof paper, and brush this with oil too.
3 To make the cake, spoon the cocoa into a basin,
add the hot water and mix them together.

4 Sieve the flour and baking powder into a large mixing bowl. Add the eggs, soft margarine, sugar and cocoa and water mixture. Using a wooden spoon, stir all this together to make a smooth mixture.

5 Spoon the cake mixture into the tin and smooth the surface. Put it in the preheated oven and bake for forty minutes, or until firm to the touch.

6 Ask an adult to help you take the cake from the oven. Turn the cake on to a wire tray and peel off the paper. Leave it to cool.

7 Make the icing by mixing the cocoa and hot water together in a bowl. Sieve in the icing sugar, add the margarine, and mix it all together with a wooden spoon.

8 Cut the cake in half vertically to make two semi-circles. Sandwich the halves together with a little of the icing, and trim one end to a point to make a nose. Put the cake on a flat board and spread the rest of the icing over the cake. Smooth the nose and face and make marks in the icing with the prongs of a fork all over the 'body', from head to tail.

9 To decorate the hedgehog, cut the almonds into strips and stick them all over the hedgehog to represent spikes, with the upper ends pointing towards the tail. Stick the glacé cherry in place for the nose, and the sweets for the eyes.

7
Chocolate Games

Chocolate is not only fun to eat, it can also provide hours of fun, with hilarious chocolate games such as Chinese Chocolate Drops.

Chinese Chocolate Drops
(for any even number of players)

Each player needs six chocolate drops and a pair of chopsticks. If you haven't got any chopsticks, use the handles of two spoons or two forks. For a party, it's best to divide into two teams, but with

smaller numbers — say between two and six — you can compete individually.

Set out the chocolate drops in little piles around the edge of a large table, one pile for each player. On the word 'go', players rush up to their chocolate drops and eat them one by one with the chopsticks. In an individual contest, the first person to finish wins, but in a team game, as soon as one player finishes the next rushes up to eat his or her chocolate drops, and so on until one team finishes and wins.

'I Like Chocolate Because . . .'
(for two or more players)

This hilarious game is a real test of wits! Everyone sits in a circle, or round a table. One person starts by choosing any letter of the alphabet, such as G, and saying 'I like chocolate because it's G . . .' the person sitting on his or her left then has to think of a suitable word beginning with G, such as 'gorgeous', or 'great', to describe chocolate.

When he or she has thought of a word, they then think of another letter of the alphabet, such as P, and say 'I like chocolate because it's P . . .' The person sitting on their left then has to think of a word, and so on, round and round the circle of players.

If you can't think of a word you are out, and the winner is the last person left in. No words must be used twice!

Floury Chocolates

(for any number of players)

You will need a plastic bowl (such as a washing-up bowl), some flour, some bibs or teatowels to tie round the players' necks, an old sheet or some newspapers and some chocolate drops.

This is a very messy game which is great fun to play, indoors or out. Begin by covering the floor with the old sheet or newspapers, then half-fill the plastic bowl with flour. Hide the chocolate drops in the bowl, place it in the middle of the sheet and tie the bibs or teatowels round the players' necks.

The object of the game is for the players to get the chocolate drops out of the bowl, using only their teeth! They should kneel by the bowl, their arms folded behind their backs, and try to get the chocolate drops. The clever players will blow the flour away to uncover the chocolates, and then pick them up with their teeth, but the silly ones will bury their faces in the flour!

Chocolates in the Circle

(for any number of players)

You will need four wrapped chocolates per player, a piece of chalk, and a piece of paper and pencil for keeping the score.

This game is suitable for playing outside where there is a hard path, or anywhere that you can draw on the floor with chalk. Begin by drawing a chalk circle, about 20 centimetres in diameter, at one end of the path. Draw a chalk line about 3 metres away from the circles. Players take it in turns to kneel down behind the chalk line and slide their four chocolates along the path, aiming for the chalk circle. When everyone has had a turn, collect up the chocolates and start again. Keep a record of how many chocolates each player manages to get into the circle, and the first person to score 20 is the winner. Anyone who puts their knees over the chalk line is disqualified.

Backwards and Forwards Chocolate Race

(for any even number of players)

You will need four plates and twice as many wrapped chocolates as there are players.

Put half the chocolates on one plate, and half on another. Divide the players into two teams – they should stand sideways in two lines facing each other. Put two plates on the floor at the head of each team, one with chocolates on and one empty.

When you say 'Go!' the first person in each team picks up a chocolate and passes it to the second person, who passes it to the third and so on. Then the last person in the line begins to pass it back, but behind his back, and so on up the line again. When the first person in the team has the chocolate again, they put it on the empty plate. They then pick up a second chocolate from the full plate, and start to pass it down the line again, and so on until all the chocolates have been transferred from one plate to the other.

The winning team is the one that transfers all its chocolates first.

Hidden Chocolate

(for any number of players)

You will need paper and a pencil.

Before the game begins, write the word CHOCOLATE in large letter on as many pieces of paper as there are players. Then cut up all the pieces of paper into single letters and hide them all over the room.

When the game starts, explain to the players that you've hidden a word in pieces. Tell them how many letters are in the word, but not what the word is. You'll have to tell them there are two letters 'O' and two 'C's in the word. They must then hunt for the letters and when they've found all nine they must make them up into the right word. The first person to work out what the word is is the winner.

Chocolate in the Bottle

(for any number of players)

You will need an upright chair, a clean empty bottle, such as a milk bottle, and some chocolate drops or chocolate peanuts. This game can be played indoors or out.

Put the chair in the middle of the room, and stand the bottle behind it. Divide the chocolate drops equally between the players. Each person then takes it in turn to stand in front of the chair and drop the chocolates over the back of the chair into the bottle. The winner is whoever gets the most chocolate drops into the bottle. Anyone who knocks down the chair is disqualified!

Chocolate Raisin Relay

(for six or more players)

You will need at least three small boxes of chocolate raisins, two bowls and teaspoons.

Divide the players into two teams, and choose a captain for each team. Give each player a teaspoon, and divide the chocolate raisins between the two bowls. Each team then lines up, with a bowl of chocolate raisins at the head of the team. On the command 'Go!' the captain of each team picks up three raisins with his teaspoon, feeds them to the player immediately behind him and runs to the back of the team.

The second player now puts three raisins on to her teaspoon and feeds them to the player behind her. The game continues until the captain is back at the front of his team, and the winners are the first team to finish.

Chocolate Duel
(for two or more players)

You will need two dessertspoons or tablespoons per player, and one chocolate per player.

Pairs of players stand facing each other, holding an empty spoon in their right hand and a spoon with a chocolate in it in their left hand. On the command 'Go!' the players use the spoon in their right hand to try and knock the chocolate out of the spoon in their partner's left hand. The winner is the first person to succeed in knocking their partner's chocolate to the floor without losing their own.

Blind Man's Chocolates
(for two or more players)

You will need half as many sweets or bars of chocolate as you have players, so if you have ten players you will need five sweets or bars of chocolate.

Before you start the game, wrap up the sweets or bars of chocolate into *small* parcels, disguising the shapes so that people can't guess what's inside. Then find an equal number of fairly *large* objects – say a shoebox full of stones, an old slipper, a bath sponge – and wrap them up too.

When the game begins, blindfold each player and put all the parcels in a pile on the floor in the middle of the room. Lead the players one by one to the pile. Ask them to choose a parcel. When everyone has chosen one, they can take off the blindfolds and unwrap their parcel.

Now you can all have a good laugh at the greediest people who have chosen the largest parcels, and are rewarded with a load of old rubbish, while those who have chosen the smallest ones are rewarded with a scrumptious sweet or bar of chocolate!

Hunt the Chocolate

(for two or more players)

This enjoyable game is a variation on Hunt the Thimble but a chocolate is used instead. You will need one wrapped chocolate.

Ask all the players to leave the room and shut the door. Then find a good hiding place for the chocolate. It must be placed somewhere in sight, but not in an obvious place.

Ask all the players to come back in the room and hunt for the chocolate. When one of them sees it they mustn't say anything but must sit down quietly. One by one the players will sit down. They mustn't give the game away by looking at the chocolate! The last person to find the chocolate is the loser. The first person is the winner and is rewarded with the chocolate!

Chocolate Zoo
(for two or more pairs of players)

For this hilarious chocolate hunt you will need lots of wrapped chocolates.

Before the game begins, hide the chocolates all over the house. You can also play this game outside, in which case hide them all over the garden. The players form pairs, and you tell each pair what animal noises they must make – 'miaow' if they are cats, 'squawk' if they are parrots, 'baa' if they are sheep, 'roar' if they are lions, and so on. When everyone knows what animals they are, send one of each pair off to look for the chocolates. Each time the hunter finds a chocolate, she makes her animal noise, and her partner goes to find her, picks up the chocolate and stays where he is. The hunter then goes to find another chocolate, and when she finds one she calls again.

After ten minutes, the two people with the most

chocolates are the winners, and they can eat all their chocolates!

Chocolate Nibbles
(for any number of players)

You will need as many long unwrapped chocolate sticks as there are players, and pieces of string.

Tie the pieces of string securely round the chocolate sticks, and hang up the strings so the chocolates are just within reach of the players' mouths! The players must try to eat their sticks of chocolate without using their hands. The first player to succeed in eating the whole of a stick is the winner.

Pass the Chocolate
(for any number of players)

You will need a bar of chocolate or box of chocolates, wrapped up in lots of layers of paper, and some form of music such as a radio or cassette player, or a piano and a pianist!

All the players sit round in a ring, and someone puts on the music. While the music is playing the parcel of chocolate is passed from one player to the next, but as soon as the music stops the player holding the parcel takes off one layer of wrapping paper. When the music starts again, the parcel must be passed on, and when it stops another layer of paper is removed, and so on. The player who takes off the last layer of paper is the winner, and is awarded the chocolate as a prize.

Name That Chocolate

(for two or more players)

For this game you will need a collection of different choclates, a blindfold and a pencil and paper.

Collect together an assortment of chocolates with different flavours, such as orange, mint, plain and milk chocolate, white chocolate, strawberry flavour, and so on. Cut them up into small pieces so there are enough for each player to taste, but don't give them too much — you want to make their task as difficult as possible!

The players wait in another room and one by one they come in and are blindfolded at the door. Sit them down and then give them their samples of chocolate, keeping a record of how many they guess correctly and how many incorrectly. The player who guesses the most right is the winner.

Chocolate Balancing Act

(for two or more players)

This is an indoors game because you need a staircase on which to play! You will also need an old but heavy book, a paper plate and some chocolate drops.

Put the chocolate drops on the paper plate, and the plate on top of the book. Then balance the book on the head of the first player. The object of the game is to walk up the stairs without dropping the plate of chocolate drops. You must keep

your hands by your sides at all times. Each player takes it in turn to see how far upstairs they can walk, and the winner is whoever manages to get the furthest. If everyone is very clever and reaches the top of the stairs, then they must start to walk down again.

Mouthwatering Memory Game

(for two or more players)

You will have to do a bit of preparation before you can play this game, but since it involves collecting lots of different wrappers from chocolates and chocolate bars, the preparation should be great fun. You will need about twenty different wrappers, a tray, and a pencil and piece of paper for each player.

Before the game starts, spread out the chocolate wrappers on the tray so they can all be seen. When the game begins, let each player look at the tray for twenty seconds. Then take the tray out of the room. Give each player a pencil and a piece of paper. The object of the game is for them to write down as many of the names of bars of chocolate as they can remember. After a minute, whoever has remembered the most correctly is the winner.

Smarties on the Tray

(for any number of players)

You will need ten Smarties for each player, and a small tray.

Put the tray on the floor. All the players stand behind a line about three metres away from the tray, and each person takes turns to throw their Smarties on to the tray. It sounds easy, but you'll find that the Smarties bounce off the tray and it's surprisingly difficult to make them stay on! The winner is the person who gets the most Smarties on the tray.

Ten Chocolate Drop!

(for four or more players, in even numbers)

You will need twenty wrapped chocolates for this game, which sounds much simpler than it really is!

Divide the players into two teams. Each team stands in a line behind its leader. On the floor in front of each leader are ten chocolates. On the command 'Go' the leader picks up the chocolates, turns round and drops them in front of the player behind him. The second player then picks them up, turns round and drops them in front of the player behind him, and so on. When the last person in the line gets the sweets, they run to the front of their line and drop them in front of the original leader, who drops them in front of the player behind him and so on down the line again.

The game continues until the original leader is

standing at the end of the line, and has all the chocolates. He or she runs to the front of the line and shouts 'Ten chocolate drop!' The winners are the first team to finish. Warning: none of the chocolates must be lost while the game is going on!

Backwards Chocolate Bars

(for any number of players)

This is an ideal indoor game for a rainy day.

The players sit in a circle. The first person calls out the name of a well known bar of chocolate — perhaps their favourite — and the player sitting on his or her right has to try and spell it backwards in ten seconds. If they take longer than this or get any of the letters in the wrong order they are out. If they manage to spell the name correctly, it's their turn to call out the name of another chocolate bar, and the person on their right has to spell it. This continues round and round the circle, and with each round the players have one second less in which to call out the letters; so for example in the second round they have nine seconds, and so on. No chocolate bar names must be used more than once. The winner is the last person left in.

I Packed my Suitcase
(for any number of players)

In this amazing memory game, players have to remember a list of names of chocolates and chocolate bars, in the correct order!

All the players sit in a circle. The game begins with the first player saying, for example: 'I packed my suitcase and in it I put a Flake and some Smarties.' The third player then says: 'I packed my suitcase and in it I put a Flake, some Smarties and a Turkish Delight.' The fourth player carries on with: 'I packed my suitcase and in it I put a Flake, some Smarties, a Turkish Delight and some After Eights.' The game continues round and round the circle, until someone gets the list wrong or can't think of another name, when they drop out. The winner is the last person left in.

I'm Thinking of a Bar of Chocolate
(for any number of players)

This is quite an easy game, and it's great fun to play.

The first player says: 'I'm thinking of a bar of chocolate that has five letters and begins with W.' The other players have to try and guess what it is by calling out their guesses, such as 'Wispa', which is correct. You might think of a name which is two words, in which case you say 'I'm thinking of a bar of chocolate that is two words, one five letters and one three letters, the first one beginning with M.' The first player to guess 'Milky Bar' would win that round.

If you want to make the game more difficult, don't give the first letter of the name, but the third letter, or the last letter, and see how this flummoxes the other players! But you must tell them that it is the third or last letter.

When you've run out of names of bars of chocolate, try boxes of chocolates or other chocolate sweets.

Hot Chocolate!
(for any number of players)

If you're good at keeping a straight face you'll do well at this game.

One player is chosen, then all the others take turns to ask him or her lots of silly or personal questions as quickly as possible, for example 'How old are you?', 'What's your name?', 'What's your younger sister called?', 'What's your favourite food?', 'What do you use to wash your face with?', 'What do you wear on your feet when it's raining?','Where are you going on holiday this year?', and so on. To all these questions the player must answer 'Hot chocolate! and must keep a straight face. The moment he or she laughs, smiles, twitches an eyebrow or grimaces, they are out, and the player who asked the question which caused them to lose their straight face takes over.

8
Chocolate Tricks

Amaze your family and friends with these mystifying magic tricks — all involving chocolate!

Milk-shake Marvel

You will need two glasses, one filled with chocolate milk-shake, and a tea towel to put on the table to stop the glasses from slipping.

Put the glass of milk-shake on a tea towel on a table, and carefully balance another identical (but empty) glass on top of it upside down. Ask the audience if anyone can drink the chocolate milk-shake in the bottom glass without touching either glass with the hands.

Then show how it's done. Pick up the top glass by holding it between your chin and your chest, and put it down on the table. (It's best to practise doing this on your own before you perform the trick, so you can do it easily in front of the audience). You can now drink the chocolate milk-shake in the bottom glass by carefully making the glasss lean towards you by holding it with your teeth and tilting it.

Chocolate Hat Trick

(for two or more players)

For this funny trick you will need at least three hats, more if possible, and a chocolate.

Line up the hats side by side on a table, with the sweet beside them. Now tell your audience that you are going to eat the chocolate, but that if one member of the audience would like to choose a hat, you will weave a magic spell and make the chocolate reappear beneath it.

When a hat has been chosen, you put the sweet in your mouth, keeping it in your cheek. Then you say 'Abracadabra, fee fi fo fum, choco, choco, chocolate, hey presto, razzamatazz, eureka!! (or any other magic words you know), and pick up the hat and put it on. Move the chocolate on to your tongue, and stick your tongue out. Lo and behold! The chocolate has reappeared beneath the hat, but not in the way that your audience were expecting!

Chocolate Orange

For this trick you will need one hat, a large orange and a chocolate orange. Alternatively, you could use a smaller orange and a creme egg.

Begin by telling your audience that with your magical powers you are going to turn an ordinary orange into a chocolate orange (or into a chocolate creme egg). Hold up the orange and show it to your audience, demonstrating that it is a perfectly ordinary orange. Then show them the inside of the hat, proving that it is a perfectly ordinary hat with nothing hidden in it. Then, turning the hat upside down, put the orange in the hat, and feel around a bit as if you're trying to find something else. Suddenly, with a cry of delight, pull out . . . a chocolate orange, or a creme egg!

To prepare for the trick, peel the orange so the peel is in two halves. Put the chocolate orange (or the creme egg) inside the orange peel. You will have to hold the orange carefully so it doesn't fall apart, and just show it to the the audience very quickly so they don't realize its hidden secret! Take more time showing them the hat, because they will think it's a trick hat. Then, when you've put the orange in the hat, and while you're saying the magic words, pull the chocolate orange out of the peel and hold it up.

Vanishing Chocolate

You will need one wrapped chocolate or small chocolate bar, and a large handkerchief.

Hold the chocolate or chocolate bar in your hand and close your fist, so the top of the chocolate is sticking out. Cover the chocolate and your fist with the handkerchief. Now ask the audience to come up one by one and feel that the chocolate is still there. After the last person has felt it, immediately say a few magic words and take the hanky away with a grand gesture, revealing that the chocolate has vanished from sight!

You will need an accomplice in the audience for this trick, which is very simple to do: your accomplice feels the chocolate last, and secretly takes it from you. That way there really is no chocolate hidden in the handkerchief at the end of the trick!

Chocolate Milk-shake Fountain

For this trick you will need the following items: a large plastic jug, a paper cup, several absorbent dish cloths, a glass of water and some chocolate milk-shake.

Start by saying to your audience: 'Wouldn't it be incredible if this jug was a magical milk-shake fountain which could turn ordinary tap water into chocolate milk-shake!'

Then pick up the glass of water and pour it into the jug. When the glass is empty, pick up the jug and pour out a glass of chocolate milk-shake!

You will need to do some careful preparaton before performing this trick. Make sure the jug you are using is not see-through. Fill it with enough dish cloths or paper towels to soak up the glass of water. Fill the paper cup with chocolate milk-shake, and put it into the jug near the spout, with the dish cloths packed all around it. You could even tape it to the wall of the jug, near the spout. You should be able to pour the milk-shake out of the jug normally. Practise doing this in front of a mirror. When you perform the trick, make sure you pour from the jug at a sideways angle, and hold it quite high up, so the audience can't see inside the jug. It is best if they are sitting a little way away from you for this trick.

When you pour the glass of water into the jug, pour it on to the dish cloths, which will soak it up. Your audience will be completely amazed by your magic skills!

Chocolate Drops from Heaven

For this amazing magic trick you will need a
glass and two chocolate drops (such as Chocolate
Buttons or Smarties).

In this trick, you show your audience that you
can conjure up two chocolate drops out of thin air.
Holding the glass in one hand, you say the secret
magic formula (Abracadabra, chocolatini, choc-
olatina, hocus pocus, whizamazoo, or similar),
pluck a chocolate drop out of the air and drop it
into the glass. Repeat the trick with the second
chocolate drop to show the first time wasn't a
fluke.

The trick is done in the following way. It is
important that you hold the glass properly. Grip

it by the rim with two fingers inside and your thumb against the outside. The two chocolate drops are hidden under your two fingers. Pretend to look for the chocolate drops in the air, and say, 'Oh yes, I can see them now, here's one coming right my way; yes, I've caught it . . . !' Then, as you pretend to drop the chocolate drop in the glass with one hand, let one of the drops go with your other hand. It should drop to the bottom of the glass so it looks as if it's been thrown in by your other hand.

Chocolate Suspension

All you need for this trick is a glass of chocolate milk-shake and a needle.

Show your audience the glass of chocolate milk-shake to prove that it's absolutely normal. Then show them the needle, to prove that there's nothing unusual about it. Tell them that you are going to say a magic spell, and then the needle will float on the milk-shake, whereas usually it would sink straight to the bottom.

The secret of the trick is that the needle must rest completely flat on the surface of the milk-shake. It will be held up by the film on the suface of the liquid. So you must be very careful about how you drop it on the milk-shake. Practise the trick on your own before performing in front of an audience – it shouldn't take you long to work out a technique that works.

Your needle must also be absolutely dry before you begin the trick.

Mental Arithmetic

Try out this mathematical trick on one of your friends. Say to them, 'I want you to add these things up.'

'OK, what?' they reply. You say,
'One tonne of chocolate,
one tonne of sawdust,
one tonne of rubbish
one tonne of fruit,
one tonne of nuts,
one tonne of bone,
one tonne of fat.
Have you got all that in your head?'
'Yes,' they reply.
'I thought so!' you answer.

Sweet Secrets

Pass a secret message to a friend using a chocolate bar! Write the message on a small piece of paper, and slide it under the paper wrapper of a chocolate bar, or unwrap a chocolate sweet, wrap the message round the sweet, and then replace the sweet's original wrapper again. No one will ever know your secret!

Disappearing Chocolate Drop

Amaze your family and friends with this clever magic trick. It's best to perform it standing behind a table with a drawer in it. All you need is a chocolate drop or a Smartie, a piece of paper and a pair of scissors.

Say to your audience, 'I'm going to make this chocolate drop disappear forever, before your very eyes. I take this piece of paper and wrap the chocolate drop in it.' Ask a member of your audience to feel the chocolate drop wrapped inside the piece of paper. Then say, 'Now I'm going to take this pair of scissors and I'm going to cut the paper and the chocolate drop into tiny little pieces. Abracadabra, the chocolate drop has completely vanished!'

This is how you do the trick. The secret lies in how you wrap up the chocolate drop, so you must do this correctly. Practise several times on your own before you perform in front of an audience, like all the best magicians. Place the chocolate drop in the centre of the piece of paper. Fold the right and left sides in, over the chocolate drop. Then fold the top third down, over the chocolate drop. As you do so, slide the chocolate drop down towards the open end of the paper. Then fold over the lower third part of the paper, too.

When the member of the audience has felt the chocolate drop wrapped in the paper, let the chocolate drop slide out of the paper into your right hand, and keep it in the palm of your hand. Put the paper in your left hand, and as you reach across the table to pick up the scissors, drop the chocolate down behind the table, into the partly-open drawer. Then cut up the paper, to the complete astonishment of your audience!

Where's the Chocolate?

This is a wonderful trick to play on your friends. All you need is one chocolate, preferably one in a wrapper.

Take the chocolate and show it to all your friends. Now tell them that you are going to put it somewhere in the room where everyone except your chosen victim can see it. You are going to hypnotize your victim so that he or she won't be able to see the chocolate, no matter how hard they look.

Choose a victim and wave the chocolate in front of the eyes a couple of times. Say, 'You are getting sleepy. You will not be able to see this chocolate although everyone else in the room can. You are getting tired; your eyelids are feeling heavy . . .!' Then put the chocolate right on top of your victim's head. Sure enough, everyone else will be able to see it but not the victim!

Favourite Feasts

For this brilliant mind-reading trick you will need a pencil, small pieces of paper (as many as you have players), and a hat or a small box.

Ask your audience, one by one, to whisper in your ear the name of their favourite chocolate bar or box of chocolates. As they tell you, write down the name on a small piece of paper, fold it in two and put it in the box.

Then you ask one person to pick a name from the box and read it without telling you what it is. (They can show it to the others.) You think carefully for a few seconds, then amaze everyone by telling them the name.

The trick is not to let anyone see what you write on the pieces of paper. In fact you only write down *one* name, the first one chosen, over and over again. So all the names on the pieces of paper are exactly the same!

How Many Smarties?

Another amazing mind-reading trick, for which you will need a tube of Smarties or some chocolate drops. You will also need a secret partner or accomplice, but none of the rest of your audience must know about this.

The trick begins with you telling everyone that you have miraculous mind-reading powers, and that you will prove it by going out of the room while everyone else divides the Smarties up between them. They should have the same number of Smarties each, between one and ten, which they must not let you see.

You come back in, and tell everyone to think very hard of the number of Smarties they have.

You go from person to person, putting your hands on either side of their heads while you concentrate very hard, trying to read their minds. When you have been round everyone in the room, amaze them all by announcing the correct number.

This is how the trick works. When you come to your secret partner, make sure you put your hands on their temples (on each side of the forehead). When they clench their teeth, their temples move very slightly. (Practise this beforehand to see how it works.) So if the number of Smarties is three, they should clench their teeth three times and you will feel their temples move three times. No one else will notice this slight movement, and the other players will be astounded by your mystifying mind-reading powers!

9
Chocolate Challenges

Puzzle yourself and your friends with this perplexing selection of chocolate mindbenders and brainteasers.

Chocolate-box Mix up

Somebody at the chocolate factory has muddled up all the names of the chocolates in this box. Can you unscramble them and find out what they all are?

GEDUF
MUR FERUTLF
DOLMAN LAMCARE
ZIPMARAN
WEBRATSRRY EREMC
FETEOF
ACRELMA
GROANE MEERC
THENLUAZ RIWHL
FECEOF EMECR
HATECLOCO RAILEC
RANTACKCURBL CEERM

Cocoa Confusion

If you were given a 5-litre container and a 3-litre container, how could you measure out 1 litre of cocoa without pouring any away?
You have an unlimited supply of cocoa to help you work out the puzzle!

Train Teaser

You are on a train which is travelling at 90 kilometres per hour. You throw a bar of chocolate 1 metre straight up in the air. Where does it land?

Chocolate Munchies

Delectable is a word that means delicious, delightful and highly enjoyable, and it's perfect for describing your favourite chocolate. Do you know the meanings of the words given below, all of which are concerned with chocolate in one way or another?

1 What is TO MUNCH?
Is it: **a** to ferment the cocoa bean
     b to be sick
     c to eat
     d to buy?

2 What is SCRUMPTIOUS?
Is it: **a** a type of chocolate
     b delicious
     c something that happens in a game of rugby
     d horrible?

3 What is CRACKNEL?

Is it: **a** a type of cup that cocoa is served in

b an insane person

c a sudden sharp noise made when toffee is cooling

d a hard, brittle toffee?

4 What is a SOUFFLÉ?

Is it: **a** a sudden wind

b the French name for chocolate

c a thermometer used when cooking chocolate

d a fluffy pudding which can be flavoured with chocolate?

5 Who is/was MONTEZUMA?

Is/was he:**a** the current king of Ghana

b the last Aztec king of Mexico

c the man who brought the first cocoa seeds to Ghana

d the man who introduced chocolate to Spain?

6 What is a MACHETE?

Is it: **a** a long, sharp knife used to cut cocoa pods from the trees

b a type of matchstick

c the pod of the cocoa bean

d the scientific name for the cocoa tree?

7 What is PRALINE?

Is it: **a** a fertilizer used for cocoa trees

b a chocolate centre made of nuts and sugar

c a type of ship used by Hernando Cortez when he visited Mexico

d a dark, bitter type of chocolate?

8 What is a FLORENTINE?

Is it: **a** the flower of the cacao tree

  b a type of boat

  c a cocoa farm in Italy

  d a type of biscuit made with chocolate and dried fruit?

9 What is a CHOCOHOLIC?

Is it: **a** a chocolate drink

  b a type of chocolate bar

  c a person who loves chocolate

  d a type of chocolate ice cream?

10 What is a MOUSSE?

Is it: **a** a type of rodent that eats cocoa beans

  b a pudding that can be flavoured with chocolate

  c an animal used to guard cocoa plantations

  d a mould used for making chocolates?

Scrambled Chocolate

Use your brains to unscramble these ten
sentences and find out what they say.

1 Scrumptious eclairs chocolate are.
2 Easter Easter eggs like on I Day.
3 Cream gateau of a I please have may piece
   chocolate with.
4 Secret of store behind chocolates the
   woodshed the is.
5 Sweets are favourite my Smarties.
6 Ermyntrude's drink drinking my chocolate
   Auntie favourite is.
7 Day of chocolates likes a mother on my
   Mother's box.
8 Bed of cup always go before I cocoa to have a
   I.
9 Colours in Smarties different come eight.
10 Ice cream like hot day on a nothing there's
   summer's a chocolate.

Odd Sweets Out

Can you spot which are the odd ones out in this
list of scrumptious sweets?

TOPIC	ROLO
POLOS	JELLYTOTS
MUNCHIES	MALTESERS
MINTOLA	AFTER EIGHT
TOFFO	SMARTIES

Spot the Difference

Two of these mouthwatering bars of chocolate are
different from the others in some way. Can you
spot which ones?

MILKY BAR

AERO

KIT KAT

SNICKERS

BREAKAWAY

BOURNVILLE

TOFFEE CRISP

DAIRY MILK

WHOLE NUT

GOLDEN CUP

Chocolate Calculations

At Charlie Chippendale's Chocolate Shop in
Chesterfield you can buy three chocolate bars and
one chocolate ice-lolly for the same price as two
chocolate eggs. One chocolate bar, two chocolate
ice-lollies and three chocolate eggs will cost you a
total of 50p.

What are the prices of chocolate bars, chocolate
ice-lollies and chocolate eggs at Charlie's shop?

Chocolate Corner

An octagonal box of chocolates had a chocolate in
each corner, seven chocolates ahead of each
chocolate and a chocolate behind each chocolate.

How many chocolates were there in the box
altogether?

Brotherly Puzzler

The owner of the Chewmore Chocolate Factory had a brother who died.

The man who died didn't have any brothers, so how were the owner of the Chewmore Chocolate Factory and the man who died related?

Hidden Words

How many other words can you find hidden in the word CHOCOLATE? For example, there's late, and heat, and cheat, and there are lots more, too. If you can find ten more then you must be of average intelligence, twenty more and you must be clever, and more than thirty and you must be absolutely brilliant!

Tongue-twisters

And finally, here's a terrible tongue-twister for you to try and get your tongue round. How many times can you say it correctly in one minute?

CHUCKLING CHILDREN CHEW CHOSEN CHOCOLATES CAREFULLY.

If you can manage that one, see how many times you can say this one in a minute – any more than ten and you must be a genius!

CHEWING CHOCOLATES CAREFULLY CAUSES CAREFREE CHILDREN TO CHUCKLE.

10
Even Crazier Chocolate Chuckles

Here's another super selection of chocolate jokes to keep you chuckling!

Knock, knock.
Who's there?
Arthur.
Arthur who?
Arthur any chocolates left or have you eaten them all?

CUSTOMER: Waiter, waiter, there's a fly in my drinking chocolate!

WAITER: *Don't shout about it, madam, or they'll all want one.*

If two Smarties are company, and three are a crowd, what are four and five?
Nine

Joke Recipe: Crispy Chocolate Beetles

Wait till 1st April to write out this recipe and give it to a friend who has admired your chocolate recipes!

Ingredients
100g fresh beetles
50g margarine
2 large bars of milk chocolate
100g caster sugar
50g fine gravel
(You will also need a baking tray.)

Method
1 Wash the beetles.
2 Melt the margarine in a small saucepan and fry the beetles until they are golden brown.
3 Put the chocolate into a bowl and melt it over a pan of boiling water, making sure that it doesn't touch the water. Ask an adult to help you with this.
4 Add the sugar and gravel to the melted chocolate.

5 Stir the beetles into the melted chocolate. Pour the mixture on to a baking tray and put into the refrigerator until set.

6 Cut into squares and serve with washing-powder sauce.

CUSTOMER: Waiter, waiter, there's a fly in my cocoa!

WAITER: *Just a minute, sir, and I'll find the lifebelt.*

What did Bessie Bunter win when she managed to give up eating chocolate?

The No-Belly Prize.

Knock, knock.
Who's there?
Paul Aidy.
Paul Aidy who?
Paul Aidy, that thief has just stolen her box of chocolates.

Who wrote I LOVE CHOCOLATE CAKE?
Buster Gutt

Why did the chocolate biscuit cry?
Because its mother had been a wafer so long.

CLARA CLEAN: Thanks for inviting me round for tea. This chocolate blancmange is lovely. But why is your dog sitting watching me and wagging his tail?

DENNIS DIRTY: *I expect it's because you're eating out of his bowl.*

What is a ghost's favourite pudding?
Chocolate mousse and scream.

MOTHER MONSTER: Percival, how often must I tell you not to eat your chocolate cake with your fingers! Use a shovel as I do.

Annie came home from school complaining of a stomach-ache. 'It's because your stomach is empty,' said her mother. 'If you eat this chocolate cake and fill up your stomach the pain will go away.' And sure enough, it soon did.

A little later, her big brother Jimmy came home from the office complaining of a headache. 'It's because your head is empty,' said Annie kindly. 'Try putting something in it!'

DETECTIVE: And what were your wife's last words, Mr Meanie?
MR MEANIE: *She said, 'I don't see how they can make a profit selling this chocolate ice cream at 5p a block.'*

CUSTOMER: Waiter, waiter, there's a fly on my chocolate gateau!
WAITER: *There's no extra charge, madam.*

Knock, knock.
Who's there?
Atomic.
Atomic who?
Atomic ache is what you'll get after eating all those chocolates.

POLICEMAN: Your first two husbands died after eating poisoned chocolate cake, and your third has just broken his neck after falling off a ladder. It's all a bit suspicious, isn't it?
WIFE: *No, not really — he wouldn't eat the poisoned chocolate cake.*

CUSTOMER: Waiter, waiter, there's a fly in my drinking chocolate!
WAITER: *Don't worry, I'll phone the RSPCA at once.*

PAUL: Ouch! That cocoa has just burned my tongue!
PAULA: *Well, silly, you should have tested it before you drank it.*

A taxi driver found a carrier bag full of chocolate cake in his cab and took it to the police. They told him that if no one had claimed it after six months it would be his!

DAPHNE: Whisper something soft and sweet in my ear.
DEREK: *Melting chocolate ice cream.*

Knock, knock.
Who's there?
Philippa.
Philippa who?
Philippa cup of hot chocolate – I'm thirsty!

Should you eat twenty pieces of chocolate gateau on an empty stomach? It's better to eat them on a plate.

MRS FUSSY: This cocoa tastes terrible!
MR CARELESS: *I made it in my pyjamas.*
MRS FUSSY: No wonder it tastes so bad.

CUSTOMER: Waiter, waiter, there's a fly in my drinking chocolate!
WAITER: *Don't worry, madam, they don't drink much.*

Knock, knock.
Who's there?
Ida.
Ida who?
Ida seventeen bars of chocolate and now I feela sick.

CUSTOMER: Waiter, waiter, this cocoa tastes like paraffin!
WAITER: *You should try the drinking chocolate, sir – it tastes like petrol.*

11
All about Easter

Easter is a Christian festival, commemorating the crucifixion of Jesus and his resurrection which means his rising from the dead. It's also traditionally the time when we exchange delicious chocolate Easter eggs with our family and friends.

Easter eggs

Nowadays chocolate eggs are eaten all over the world at Easter, but they were first introduced in France, Italy, Spain and the Netherlands about 150 years ago. Eggs are associated with Easter because they represent new life. People have always seen birds hatching from eggs, and the early Christians chose the egg as a symbol of Jesus's resurrection. So eggs have always played a part in Easter celebrations.

Traditions and games

All sorts of traditions and games are associated with Easter. It used to be the time when people first wore their new spring clothes, and today, some women and girls still buy or make an attractive new 'Easter bonnet' to wear on Easter

Sunday. Parades are held with prizes for the best bonnets.

In some villages and towns, such as Preston in Lancashire, an Easter egg race is held, where eggs are rolled down a hillside. The owner of the winning egg is awarded a prize, and is traditionally supposed to have good luck for the rest of the year.

In Washington DC in the USA, children roll decorated eggs down the lawn of the president's house, the White House.

In the north of England, children go 'Pace egging' at Easter-time, begging for eggs and other presents, and sometimes put on a Pace egg play, a type of play that has been performed for hundreds of years. 'Pace eggs' means Easter eggs: the word pace comes from the French word 'Paques', meaning Easter.

Another Easter game is to hide Easter eggs in the garden, and to pretend that the Easter Bunny has visited in the night and put them there. The bunny or hare is another Easter tradition: in ancient times people used to sacrifice hares to the pagan goddess of Eostre, after which Easter is named.

How to Make a Chocolate Easter Egg

Ingredients
100g milk chocolate
(You will also need
a large egg
a needle

an egg cup
a small jug
aluminium foil
or white icing and an icing bag with a thin
nozzle
or sugar flowers with a little melted chocolate.)

Method
1 Holding the egg carefully, make a fairly large
hole in the top of the shell.
2 Shake out the yolk and white and put them
into a bowl (you can use them for cooking later).
Carefully wash out the eggshell with scalding
water (ask an adult to help you with this) and
leave it to dry out thoroughly inside.
3 Put the chocolate into a small bowl making
sure that it does not touch the water, and melt it
by putting this bowl over a larger pan of boiling
water. Ask an adult to help you with this.
4 When the chocolate has melted, pour it into the
jug.
5 Put the eggshell into an egg cup to balance it.
Pour the melted chocolate through the hole in the
eggshell, holding the eggshell so it does not fall
over.
6 Leave the egg in a cool place so that the
chocolate can set. When the egg is hard, crack off
the shell.
7 Either gift-wrap the egg in aluminium foil, or
decorate it with patterns made of white icing, or
by sticking on sugar flowers, using a little melted
chocolate to attach them.

12
Chocolatey Tales

How many of these funny books have you read?
At the bottom of page 99 there's a space for you to
add some amusing chocolatey book titles of your
own!

HOW TO MAKE CHOCOLATE CAKE
by *U. Tensils*

CHOCOLATE BLANCMANGE
by *E. Tittup*

THE MYSTERY OF THE MISSING CHOCOLATE CAKE
by *Henrietta Lott*

MY FAVOURITE SWEETS
by *Ivor Marsbar*

CHOCOLATE BUNS FOR TEA
by *Eileen Joyit*

I LOVE CHOCOLATES
by *Oliver Nutherwon*

THE UNHAPPY TEASHOP
by *Sad Café*

THE LOST BARS OF CHOCOLATE
by *Hugh Seenthem*

WHO STOLE THE CHOCOLATE ECLAIRS?
by *Howard I. Know*

EASTER CELEBRATION
by *Ivan E. Steregg*

WHERE HAVE MY CHOCOLATES GONE?
by *M. T. Cupboard*

A BAR OF WHOLENUT
by *I. M. Nutty*

Can you think of any more funny book titles that
you would find in your chocolate library? Write
them down in the space below.

13
Chocolate Quiz

Find out how much you know about your favourite sweet with this mind-boggling chocolate quiz. The answers can be found on page 111.

1 Name all the colours you'll find in a tube of Smarties.

2 Where is the headquarters of Cadbury Ltd?

3 The city of York is famous for many things, such as its beautiful minster, but it's also the home of two well known chocolate making companies. Can you name them?

4 There are two different bars of Kit Kat on sale – how many fingers are there in each?

5 Smarties celebrated an anniversary in 1987 – which one is it?

6 Can you fill in the missing letters to give the correct names of these chocolates and chocolate bars?

–IT K– –   B–EA–A–AY
M–N–H–ES   –AT–H A–ER–
–OFF–– C–IS–   –IN–OL–
–O–O   W––NU– –HIP
DRI–TE–   –F–ER –IG–T
L–O– –A–   CA––MA–-

7 Which of today's favourite chocolate bars was introduced the earliest, and when?

8 Who successfully introduced cocoa and chocolate to the Spanish court, and in which century?

9 When were cocoa and chocolate first introduced to England?

10 What were the names of the public places where cocoa and chocolate were first drunk in England?

11 What do cocoa and chocolate come from?

12 How much chocolate do people in the United Kingdom eat each week?

13 In chocolate-making, what are moulded products?

14 What is the special feature about the chocolates in a box of Black Magic?

15 What is the special feature about the chocolates in a box of Dairy Box or Milk Tray?

16 Which countries do cocoa trees grow in?

17 What other trees do cocoa trees look like?

18 What is cocoa butter?

19 What are the centres of cocoa beans known as:
a cocoa nibs
b cocoa pens
c cocoa mass
d cocoa picks?

20 What type of nuts are used in a bar of Cadbury's Whole Nut?

21 Everybody knows Cadbury's Fruit and Nut, but not everybody knows exactly what type of fruit and nuts it contains. Do you?

22 Who were the Aztecs, and what role did they play in the history of chocolate?

23 What colour is the ripe pod of the cocoa bean?

24 How many cocoa pods are needed to make 1 kilogramme of cocoa?

25 What is chocolatl?

14
Your Personal
Choco-file

Chocolate Survey

What secret chocolate-eating habits do you have? Do you like to eat chocolates under the bedclothes at midnight, by the light of a torch? Do you hoard a secret supply of your favourite chocolates, and if so, where do you keep it? Or do you like to eat your favourite chocolate bar as soon as you get it? Are you a lone chocolate eater, or do you like to munch in company?

Here's a special Top Secret Chocolate survey, where you can record your personal chocolate-eating habits.

NAME

ADDRESS

AGE

SCHOOL

MY TOP TEN FAVOURITE CHOCOLATE BARS ARE

MY FAVOURITE BOX OF CHOCOLATES IS

THE CHOCOLATE I EAT FIRST IN A BOX OF
CHOCOLATES IS

MY FAVOURITE CHOCOLATE SWEETS ARE

I PREFER MILK/PLAIN CHOCOLATE
(cross out whichever doesn't apply)

ON AVERAGE, I EAT .... INDIVIDUAL
CHOCOLATES, AND/OR .... CHOCOLATE BARS
PER DAY/WEEK

ON AVERAGE, I SPEND £ .... p PER DAY/WEEK
ON CHOCOLATE.

MY FAVOURITE CHOCOLATE BISCUITS ARE

MY FAVOURITE CHOCOLATE CAKE IS

MY FAVOURITE CHOCOLATE ICE-CREAM/LOLLY IS

I LIKE CHOCOLATE BECAUSE

MY FAVOURITE TIME TO EAT CHOCOLATE IS

MY FAVOURITE PLACE TO EAT CHOCOLATE IS

MY FAVOURITE CHOCOLATE JOKE IS

MY SECRET CHOCOLATE HIDING-PLACE IS

IF I HAD TWO CHOCOLATE BARS, I WOULD GIVE
ONE TO

THE KIND OF CHOCOLATE SWEET I WOULD
MOST LIKE MANUFACTURERS TO
PRODUCE IS

SIGNATURE

DATE

Chocolate Collection

Do you collect anything? You might have a great
collection of stamps, postcards, bus tickets or
coins, but have you ever thought of collecting
chocolate wrappers? You can add to your personal
choco-file by building up a wonderful collection of
all the different wrappers that come with the
various types of chocolate bars and other
chocolate sweets and wrappers from inside boxes
of chocolates.

If you go on holiday to a foreign country you can start an international collection of wrappers from around the world. Or if you have a penfriend who lives overseas, ask him or her to send you some wrappers from their country. You could send them some of yours in return.

Stick your wrappers in a scrap book, and write down the date you ate the chocolate bar, whether someone gave it to you and what you thought of it. Give it marks out of ten for flavour, crunchiness and so on.

As you collect wrappers over the years you will see how the designs change and new bars are brought in. Your collection will also be your chocolate-eating diary, and a record of all your favourite sweets.

Answers

Chocolate-box Mixup (p.81)

Fudge
Rum truffle
Almond caramel
Marzipan
Stawberry creme
Toffee

Caramel
Orange creme
Hazelnut whirl
Coffee creme
Chocolate eclair
Blackcurrant creme

Cocoa Confusion (p. 82)

Fill the 3-litre container and empty it into the
5-litre container. Fill the 3-litre container again
and pour the cocoa into the 5-litre container until
the 5-litre container is full. One litre will be left
in the 3-litre container.

Train Teaser (p. 82)

On the ground directly below where you threw it
from.

Chocolate Munchies (p. 82)

1c	to eat
2b	delicious
3d	a hard brittle toffee
4d	a fluffy pudding which can be flavoured with chocolate
5b	the last Aztec king of Mexico
6a	a long, sharp knife used to cut cocoa pods from the trees.
7	a chocolate centre made of nuts and sugar
8d	a type of biscuit made with chocolate and dried fruit
9c	a person who loves chocolate
10b	a pudding that can be flavoured with chocolate

Scrambled Chocolates (p. 85)

1 Chocolate eclairs are scrumptious.
2 I like Easter eggs on Easter Day.
3 Please may I have a piece of chocolate gateau with cream.
4 The secret store of chocolates is behind the woodshed.
5 My favourite sweets are Smarties.
6 Drinking chocolate is my Auntie Ermyntrude's favourite drink.
7 My mother likes a box of chocolates on Mother's Day.
8 I always have a cup of cocoa before I go to bed.
9 Smarties come in eight different colours.
10 There's nothing like a chocolate ice-cream on a hot summer's day.